KES...

Length:
32 - 35cms
(12 - 14ins)

Wingspan:
71- 80cms
(28 - 32ins)

Weight:
0.14 - 0.31kg
(5oz - 11oz)

Habitat:
Kestrels do not build their own nests but use holes & forks in trees, scrapes on the ground, ledges on cliffs & buildings and old nests of other birds. Because of this ability, Kestrels are able to exploit a wide range of habitat.

Photo:
R Wilmshurst

Despite being persecuted during the 19th century when gamekeepers virtually eliminated it from some parts of the British Isles, the Kestrel has made a remarkable comeback and it now numbers about 60,000 pairs - more than all of our other diurnal raptors put together.

One of the reasons for this recovery is the Kestrel's remarkable adaptability. It has learned to take advantage of new hunting areas such as roadsides and even town centres. It is also able to switch to different prey whenever occasional slumps in the vole population occur.

Although the Kestrel is a true Falcon, its flight-style, prey and method of hunting are far from typical. The Kestrel feeds mainly on small mammals – principally the short tailed vole – which it hunts by hovering, head into wind; or which it spots from a perch.

Mature male Kestrels are easily distinguished from females, being a warm red-brown colour with a grey head and tail. The female is mainly brown with darker speckles and bars, and is slightly larger with a wingspan of over 31ins.

MERLIN
falco columbarius

Length:
25 - 30cms
(10 - 12ins)

Wingspan:
50 - 62cms
(20 - 24ins)

Weight:
0.12 - 0.30kg
(4oz - 11oz)

Habitat:
Open upland country. Hilly areas offer the best vantage points. Nests frequently in patches of heather. Some birds have recently taken to the forest margins.

Photo:
B S Turner

Britain's 1,300 Merlin pairs represent about 95% of the total European population. It is a population which continues to decline: the reasons for the fall are not fully understood but, since the Merlin is a predominantly ground-nesting bird which preys largely on small birds, two of the major factors would secondary pesticide poisoning.

Ironically, Britain's northern grouse moors seem to offer this bird its best chance of survival, but only if the Merlin is allowed to live free of persecution by gamekeepers.

The Merlin is Britain's smallest falcon with a maximum wingspan of only 2ft, but it is probably the most active. It does not stoop on its prey but chases it down in high speed pursuit, rising above the prey at the last instant to strike downwards with its talons.

HOBBY
falco subbuteo

Length:
30 - 36cms
(12 - 14ins)

Wingspan:
82 - 92cms
(32 - 36ins)

Weight:
0.13 - 0.34kg
(4oz - 12oz)

Habitat:
Heath and downland,
provided there are
some tall trees for
nesting. Hobbies do
not build nests but use
abandoned crow,
magpie & sparrow-
hawk nests or even
squirrel dreys

Photo:
F W Lane.

From a conservation standpoint, the Hobby is one of the Raptor world's more recent success stories — the UK population has increased significantly over recent years and it can now be seen in greater numbers.

The heath and downlands of southern Britain are at the extreme northern edge of the Hobby's range and between 100 & 200 pairs visit this country to breed between late April and late August each year before returning to Africa for the winter.

The Hobby is an extremely active and dashing little Falcon which specialises in catching large insects and small birds, especially housemartins and swifts which it takes in high speed, surprise attacks.

Hobbies are particularly active at dusk and have even been known to hunt large insects and bats by moonlight. Like most Falcons, Hobbies do not build nests but instead, take over the disused nests of other birds, mainly rooks, crows and magpies.

GYRFALCON
falco rusticolus

The beautiful Gyrfalcon is the world's largest falcon. It can have a wingspan in excess of 5ft and weigh up to 4lbs 10oz. Their plumage is highly variable, ranging from brown and grey, to almost pure white with a few black spots.

Being a bird of the Arctic tundra, Gyrs are not resident in this country and few visit us: however, they do so with sufficient regularity to be regarded as British migrants.

Gyrs usually appear in the Northern Isles during November/December and March/April, and are sometimes seen in Ireland, the West Country and the Scilly Isles. It is mainly the almost pure white Greenland and Canadian races of Gyr which visit us, the darker Icelandic and Scandinavian races being largely non-migratory.

Prey consists almost entirely of birds which – as well as stooping – it can fly down in direct pursuit (the Gyr is the world's fastest Falcon in level flight). It can use its superior weight and speed to tackle quite large birds such as geese and large sea-birds, but inland populations rely almost entirely on Grouse and Ptarmigan.

Length:
50 - 60cms
(20 - 24ins)

Wingspan:
130 - 160cms
(51 - 63ins)

Weight:
0.8 - 2.1kg
(1lb 12oz - 4lbs 10oz)

Habitat:
Rocky coasts and low-lying moorland where prey is plentiful

Photo:
E & D Hosking

PEREGRINE FALCON

falco peregrinus

During the hey-day of falconry the Peregrine was a highly prized and protected bird, but with the introduction of effective sporting guns, the practice of falconry declined. So the persecution of the Peregrine began, as the interests of the bird came into direct conflict with those of the game-shooter.

This persecution continued into the 20th century and, although other Raptor populations were able to recover when game-keeping was suspended during the 2 world wars, Peregrines continued to be victimised on the grounds that they killed carrier pigeons. Today, however, the population is recovering and Britain's 1,200 pairs – now often seen at sites not used for over 100 years – make up a very important part of the European population.

Peregrines are exclusively bird-eaters who take their prey in flight, either binding to the victim after a short chase in level flight or – more often – by climbing above the prey and stooping at speeds of up to 150 mph, striking with the hind talon and usually with sufficient force to kill outright.

The Peregrine is the largest of Britain's breeding Falcons (the larger Gyrfalcon is an occasional, non-breeding, visitor). Female Peregrines have a wingspan in excess of 40ins and weigh almost 3lbs, while males (tiercels) weigh about a third less.

Length:
36 - 48cms
(14 - 19 ins)

Wingspan:
95 - 110cms
(37 - 43ins)

Weight:
0.58 - 1.3kg
(1lb 4oz - 2lbs 14oz)

Habitat:
Rocky crags both coastal & inland. Sometimes found in forested areas but more commonly in open country.
No nests are built but eggs are laid directly onto rocky ledges and, sometimes, even on tall buildings.

Photo:
E & D Hosking

SPARROWHAWK

accipiter nisus

Length:
28 - 38cms
(11 - 15ins)

Wingspan:
55 - 70cms
(22 - 28ins)

Weight:
0.11 - 0.34kg
(4oz - 12oz)

Habitat:
Mixed woodland with some open spaces and paths. The Sparrowhawk has adapted to using urban parks and large gardens, especially during the winter. Nests are built in tall trees.

Photo:
A R Hamblin

Although the Sparrowhawk shared the severe decline of other British Raptors (resulting from persecution and the advent of organochlorines), it has made a remarkably rapid recovery and is now estimated to number about 30,000 pairs.

A rather small bird with short, broad wings, a long tail and long, slender legs, the Sparrowhawk is ideally suited to life in woodland.

The Sparrowhawk preys on small birds and uses its great agility to pursue its prey through woodland at high speed. However, it is sometimes so intent on its prey that it collides with trees and other obstacles: many are killed or injured in this way.

Sparrowhawks can carry prey as large as themselves (the female is 25% larger than the male, with a wingspan of up to 28ins.) and will frequently take their kills to a favourite post to be plucked.

GOSHAWK
accipiter gentilis

In Great Britain the Goshawk was shot, poisoned and trapped to extinction during the 19th century by gamekeepers. Whilst it is true that the Goshawk is a formidable predator, most of this prejudice (which still exists today) was based on an exaggerated opinion of its powers.

Of the two British species of true Hawk (accipiters), the Goshawk is by far the largest being up to 6 times heavier than the Sparrowhawk. A large Gos can weigh over 4 lbs and have a wingspan in excess of 5ft. It is predominantly a woodland bird and has adapted to living in conifer plantations where, to its great credit, the Forestry Commission is actively protecting known nest sites.

The Gos is completely fearless and will take quarry on the ground or in the air. It is capable of remarkable speeds over distances of up to 500m with deep, rapid beats of its comparatively short, broad wings.

Prey ranges from songbirds to hares. Victims are grasped with large, powerful feet and held with increasing pressure, driving in the long, sharp talons until all movement ceases. Current estimates are for a UK Goshawk population of about 300 pairs.

Length:
48 - 62cms
(18 - 25ins)

Wingspan:
135 - 165cms
(53 - 65ins)

Weight:
0.62 - 2.05kg
(1lb 6oz - 4lbs 8oz)

Habitat:
Woodland (both deciduous and coniferous) with open glades and breaks for hunting. Nests in trees, sometimes refurbishing existing nests but, in conifer plantations, always building a new one.

Photo:
H Schrempp

OSPREY
pandion haliaetus

Length:
55 - 58cms
(21 - 23ins)

Wingspan:
145 - 170cms
(57 - 70ins)

Weight:
1.1 - 2kg
(2lbs 8oz - 4lbs 8oz)

Habitat:
Coasts and near any lake, reservoir or river which is free from disturbance and where fishing is possible. Nests in trees and on artificial platforms.

Photo:
Ron Austing

Persecuted to extinction in Britain by 1917, the comeback of the Osprey started in 1959 when a pair bred successfully at Loch Garten in Scotland. This site, now under the permanent protection of the R.S.P.B., attracts more than 70,000 human visitors each year.

The Osprey is a migratory bird which spends the winter in Africa, but each year about 110 pairs return to Scotland to breed.

Although it will sometimes feed on other small prey, the Osprey is a specialist fish-eater and will plunge into the water from about 30ft, sometimes becoming completely submerged in its quest for food.

Ospreys' feet are specifically adapted to catch fish. They have long, sharp, very curved talons and the undersides of the feet are covered in tiny spikes. Ospreys are also able to turn their outer toes to the rear, so giving them two opposing pairs of talons. Among diurnal Raptors, this ability is unique.

Compared to a body weight of up to 4.5lbs, the Osprey has very large wings with a span of almost 6ft. These it uses to lift both itself and its prey – both soaking wet – from the water's surface, hanging in mid-air after a few strong wing-beats to shed water with a characteristic shake of its body, before flying off to feed.

HONEY BUZZARD

pernis apivorus

Length:
52 - 60cms
(20 - 24ins)

Wingspan:
135 - 150cms
(53 - 59ins)

Weight:
0.4 - 1kg
(15oz - 2lbs 5oz)

Habitat:
Deciduous forest and mature pine & spruce woods, where bee and wasp nests are plentiful. The Honey Buzzard builds its own nest in tall trees and usually incorporates a mass of leafy twigs.

Photo:
Philip Perry

The Honey Buzzard is a migratory breeding visitor to Britain and is only present between mid-April and mid-August: winters are spent in Africa, south of the Sahara. Despite a European summer population of about 40,000 pairs, the Honey Buzzard is a very rare bird in this country - in 1988 there were records of only 10 pairs here, although - because it is a shy woodland bird - numbers have probably been under-recorded.

Despite its name, the Honey Buzzard it is not a honey eater at all but a specialised predator of wasp and bee larvae. It detects nests by observing the movements of the insects whilst soaring or hovering above, and then digs out the larvae from the nest. The Honey Buzzard has special adaptations to cope with this particular food source. Scale-like feathers on forehead and cheeks protect it from stings whilst a long, narrow head enable it to investigate comparatively small holes in the ground: the Honey Buzzard's feet are adapted for digging, having short blunt talons and thick scales; and its nostrils are thin slits, less prone to being clogged with soil.

The Honey Buzzard can supplement its diet with small mammals, birds, eggs and invertebrates and will even eat fruit and berries.

MARSH HARRIER

circus aeruginosus

In addition to the twin hazards of persecution and toxic chemical attack endured by our other Raptors, the Marsh Harrier has been particularly affected by habitat loss due mainly to land drainage. Consequently the Marsh Harrier effectively became extinct in Britain by 1917.

During the following few years there were occasional attempts by immigrant birds from Holland to breed in the East Anglian reed-beds. Howeverit was not until 1927 - when Lord Desborough, and later the Norfolk Naturalists' Trust, gave them protection - that the population of Marsh Harriers began its painfully slow recovery, now numbering about 110 pairs in the UK.

As its name suggests, the Marsh Harrier is a wetland bird, nesting in dense reed-beds or other thick vegetation in shallow water. It feeds mainly on other marsh birds including duck and waders, but will also take small mammals. Prey is usually caught by surprise as the Harrier quarters the ground, using all available cover.

It is the largest of our Harriers, with a wingspan of over 4ft and weighing up to 1lb 12oz.

Length:
48 - 56cms
(19 - 22 ins)

Wingspan:
115 - 130cms
(45 - 51ins)

Weight:
0.4 - 0.8kg
(14oz - 1lb 12oz)

Habitat:
Wetlands where disturbance is minimal. Large dense reedbeds are essential for nesting.

Photo:
E & D Hosking

HEN HARRIER

circus cyaneus

Length:
44 - 52cms
(17 - 21ins)

Wingspan:
100 - 120cms
(39 - 47ins)

Weight:
0.3 - 0.7kg
(10oz - 1lb 9oz)

Habitat:
Prefers open lowlands including bogs, moors, heaths and marshes, but has adapted to young conifer plantations. Nests are always on the ground and in cover.

Photo:
John Hawkins

During the breeding season, Britain's indigenous population of Hen Harriers is concentrated in upland Scotland, Ireland and Wales but during the winter the population disperses to coastal regions including East Anglia and south-east England.

The difference in appearance between mature male and female Hen Harriers is striking, the males being a soft dove-grey with white rumps, and females having dark brown upper parts and yellow-brown underparts.

Along with many other British Birds of Prey, the Hen Harrier population has declined drastically, partly due to loss of its heath, moor and marshland habitat. The population has also shrunk as a result of persecution by gamekeepers on grouse moors and now stands at about 650 pairs.

With a wingspan of almost 4 ft and weighing up to 1lb 9oz, the Hen Harrier hunts its prey of small mammals and ground nesting birds, by low-level systematic searching. For this it uses its superb hearing aided by an owl-like facial disk, and utilises all available cover to gain the advantage of surprise.

MONTAGU'S HARRIER
circus pygargus

Of similar size to the Hen Harrier but more lightly built, Montagu's Harrier is the UK's rarest breeding Raptor. It narrowly missed total extinction early this century, at which time the population was confined mainly to the Norfolk Broads.

That the Montagu has survived at all is largely due to a shift from its normal habitat to the use of crop fields (mainly cereal) for nesting. Also, co-operation between farmers and conservation organisations has played a part. As a result, the Montagu has now established new territory in south west Britain. A purely migrant visitor, present only between April and September, there have been years when no breeding pairs have appeared. However, in 1990, 12 pairs reared a total of 22 young.

The diet of Montagu's Harrier is extremely varied and includes small mammals, song birds, invertebrates, reptiles, amphibians, and the chicks and eggs of ground-nesting birds. Normal hunting flight is a series of slow glides punctuated with strong, rapid wingbeats. This extremely buoyant bird is capable of rapid changes of direction and sudden stoops. Unlike other harriers, Montagu's can fly fast enough to chase fast-moving ground prey and can even take small birds in flight.

Length:
43 - 47cms
(17 - 19ins)

Wingspan:
105 - 120cms
(41 - 47ins)

Weight:
0.23 - 0.44kg
(8oz - 1lb)

Habitat:
Lowland regions - marshes, sand dunes, young forestry plantations and heaths. More recently, nesting in arable crops. Nests are always built on the ground, usually in tall vegetation including growing crops.

Photo:
John Hawkins

RED KITE
milvus milvus

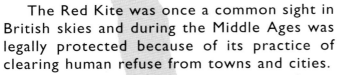

The Red Kite was once a common sight in British skies and during the Middle Ages was legally protected because of its practice of clearing human refuse from towns and cities.

Unfortunately the Red Kite was also a major predator of domestic fowl and this led to its relentless persecution. By 1905 the total British population was reduced to only 12 birds.

Today, the Red Kite is once again a protected species and, with the introduction of birds imported from Sweden and Spain, its numbers have increased to almost 110 pairs in the UK. Most of the Kite population is currently confined to Wales but efforts are being made to reintroduce it to some parts of its old English ranges.

With a wingspan of almost 6ft 6ins, a slender body and long forked tail, the Red Kite is our most elegant Bird of Prey and one of the most skilled in flight. It will eat almost anything (dead or alive) and will often steal food from other Birds of Prey.

Length:
60 - 66cms
(23 - 26ins)

Wingspan:
175 - 195cms
(69 - 77ins)

Weight:
0.76 - 1.6kg
(1lb 11oz - 3lb 8oz)

Habitat:
Roosting and nesting in valleys containing ancient oakwoods, but hunting over heath and moorland. Lowland pastures and wetlands are also used during winter.

Photo:
J. Hawkins

COMMON BUZZARD
buteo buteo

Length:
51 - 57cm
(20 - 22ins)

Wingspan:
113 - 128cm
(44 - 50ins)

Weight:
0.4 - 1.4kg
(15oz - 3lbs)

Habitat:
Buzzards build their nests in trees and sometimes on rocky ledges. When breeding they favour woodland with some open ground, but will also live on open moorland provided there are some trees

Photo:
J. Hawins

The Common Buzzard is a medium sized Raptor with a maximum wingspan of just over 4ft. Weighing up to 3lbs, it has broad, rounded wings and a fairly short tail which it uses to soar and glide effortlessly over hills and valleys. However, in direct flapping flight the Common Buzzard's movements can appear quite laboured and it prefers to still-hunt from a convenient perch, gliding down to seize prey in its talons.

The history of the Common Buzzard shows the usual pattern of persecution which has driven it into western Britain, particularly the West Country, Wales and Scotland. However, during the late 1950s and early 1960s, Buzzard numbers were dramatically reduced still further when myxomatosis wiped out 99% of the rabbit population, so depriving it of its major source of food.

However, being an adaptable bird the Buzzard has since been able to exploit other sources of food including voles, young birds, amphibians, reptiles and invertebrates, and is now beginning to re-colonise its old range.

The British population of Common Buzzards is now estimated at 20,000 pairs.

ROUGHLEGGED BUZZARD

buteo lagopus

The Roughlegged Buzzard is so named because of the covering of feathers which extends down its legs as far as its toes. It is a bird of the northern tundra, where it breeds during the summer, migrating further south to winter quarters. Britain is at the extreme western end of its migration range, but the Eastern Counties of England and Scotland receive a number of these birds in October and November each year.

The breeding and migration cycle of the Roughlegged Buzzard is dependent on the small mammal population which comprises the bulk of its diet. Lemmings are especially important. During years of glut, Buzzards breed freely during the summer and so, when the winter mammal population declines, large numbers of juveniles disperse southwards, resulting in large influxes into the UK. The winter of 1994/5 was a particularly good year.

The Roughlegged Buzzard is slightly larger than the Common Buzzard which it closely resembles, having a wingspan of almost 5ft and weighing over 3.5 lbs. Females in this species are only slightly larger than males.

Length:
50 - 60cms
(19 - 24ins)

Wingspan:
120 - 150cms
(47 - 59ins)

Weight:
0.7 - 1.6kg
(1lb 8oz - 3lbs 10oz)

Habitat:
Low lying tundra, but winter visitors to Britain favour moor-land, wetlands, farm land and dunes.

Photo:
Ron Austing

GOLDEN EAGLE

aquila chrysaetos

Length:
75 - 88cm
(30 - 35ins)

Wingspan:
204 - 220cm
(80 - 87ins)

Weight:
2.8 - 6.7kg
(6lbs 3oz -14lbs 11oz)

Habitat:
Open mountainous land. Nests are huge structures of twigs and small branches on rocky ledges.

Photo:
Sylvestris

The Golden Eagle - its name is due to the golden crown and neck feathers - is Britain's only true or "booted" Eagle. With a wingspan which may exceed 7ft and weighing over 14lbs, it is Britain's second largest Bird of Prey after the White-Tailed Sea Eagle.

The Golden Eagle is largely confined to the mountain regions of Scotland, where it uses the strong winds and updrafts to soar effortlessly in search of its food, consisting mainly of carrion, rabbits and hares. The population is currently estimated at around 450 pairs, representing about 15% of the total European population.

Apart from persecution and disturbance, the main threats still facing the Golden Eagle result from the increasing use of land for conifer forestry, which reduces the availability of prey; and improved methods of sheep husbandry, which has resulted in a significant reduction in carrion. The latter has greatest effect during the lean winter months when sheep are driven to more sheltered lowland pasture.

WHITE TAILED EAGLE

haliaeetus albicilla

In its adult form, the White Tailed Eagle has all the hallmarks of a classic Sea or Fish Eagle. It is a large, dark bird with a contrasting white tail; its legs are unfeathered; the beak is large and powerful; and it has a loud, high-pitched call.

Slightly larger than the Golden Eagle, the White Tailed Eagle has the greatest wingspan of any British bird, spreading to almost 8ft. Females weigh about 25% more than males, and can weigh over 15 pounds. In flight, the White Tailed Eagle is easily distinguished from the Golden Eagle by its very short tail.

The White Tail was persecuted to extinction in the British Isles when, in 1918 the last survivor - an elderly female - was shot. Since then, some individuals have drifted to our shores but it was not until the late 1970s that they were successfully reintroduced on the Scottish island of Rhum from Norwegian stock, with the first breeding success following in 1985.

The White Tailed Eagle is a coastal bird and, in this country, is limited to about 10 pairs in the Western Isles of Scotland. It is an active predator, taking fish, mammals and waterbirds. It is also an eater of carrion, and will steal food from other Birds of Prey and gulls.

Length:
68 - 90cms
(27 - 36ins)

Wingspan:
2 - 2.4m
(6ft 6ins - 7ft 10ins)

Weight:
3.1 - 6.9kg
(6lbs 13oz - 15lbs 3oz)

Habitat:
Coasts and near large lakes and rivers, nesting as much as 10km inland. The White Tail builds huge nests of wood, heather and seaweed which may be 5ft across.

Photo:
W S Clark